SOULFUL CONNECTIONS

Edited by

Heather Killingray

First published in Great Britain in 2003 by
POETRY NOW
Remus House,
Coltsfoot Drive,
Peterborough, PE2 9JX
Telephone (01733) 898101
Fax (01733) 313524

All Rights Reserved

Copyright Contributors 2003

HB ISBN 0 75434 419 3
SB ISBN 0 75434 420 7

FOREWORD

Although we are a nation of poets we are accused of not reading poetry, or buying poetry books. After many years of listening to the incessant gripes of poetry publishers, I can only assume that the books they publish, in general, are books that most people do not want to read.

Poetry should not be obscure, introverted, and as cryptic as a crossword puzzle: it is the poet's duty to reach out and embrace the world.

The world owes the poet nothing and we should not be expected to dig and delve into a rambling discourse searching for some inner meaning.

The reason we write poetry (and almost all of us do) is because we want to communicate: an ideal; an idea; or a specific feeling. Poetry is as essential in communication, as a letter; a radio; a telephone, and the main criterion for selecting the poems in this anthology is very simple: they communicate.

CONTENTS

Let Me	Sharon Spencer	1
Yellow Drops	John Ball	2
Take Me In Your Arms	Angela R Davies	3
Lament	Sammy	4
You	Moira H Thorburn	6
Betrayed	Alice Higham	7
My Family Treasures	Jean Gill	8
Don't Go	G M Pilkington	9
One More Time	Susan Watson	10
On Our Anniversary	David A Reddish	11
Tell Him About It	Frances Ann Hall	12
I'll Always Love You	Maria Jenkinson	13
First Concert/First Love	Lucy Coelho	14
For Gren	Lydia Barnett	15
The Silence Of The Night	Brigitta D'Arcy	16
Untitled	Sheila Atkinson	17
Castles	Linda Landers	18
The Beach	Nina Woolf	20
Me And You	Kathryn Pope	21
My Jim	Rita Johnson	22
You Are Part Of Me	Lynda Long	23
Cymbeline	Sparky	24
True	Paula Natalie Burgess	25
Eternal Ember	B Barter	26
She Is You	Ray Smith	27
If A Smile May Tell Me	C J Bayless	28
Nothing Without You!	Gary Thompson	29
Mandy	Noel Thaddeus Lawler	30
And I Will See You In The Morning	Jonathan Pegg	31
I Love You	Sue Umanksi	32
Lonely Heart	Halima Hussain	33
You're Never Far Away	David Russell	34
Fragile Is Love	Ainsley McKenzie	35
Questions	Gary J Finlay	36
Winter's Reality	Johan Botha	37

We Don't Choose We Just Fall	Lynsey Tocker	38
Questions	Wendy-Elezabeth	40
Marriage	Trisha Matthews	41
Untitled	Donna Salisbury	42
Victoria	Sandy Laird	43
Yesterday	Marian Morgan	44
A Poem For My Mum	Nicola Barnes	46
Poem To Bill On Our 10th Wedding Anniversary	Meg Stephenson	47
My Dad	Moira Clelland	48
My Son Steven	R E Bilson	49
The Gentleman Pugilist	Linda Zulaica	50
To Kate	Angus Sinclair	51
To My Mother	Alan Wooding	52
Labour Of Love	Phil Clayton	53
Mother/Daughter, The Relationship	M Fitzpatrick Jones	54
Family Ties	Kay Astbury	55
Thank You My Spirit Child	Meg Aku Sika Millar	56
Thank You Dad	John Lewis	58
Ammâh Ennairam	Patricia Aboagye	60
Gran	N Lord	61
My Father	Jane Ward	62
From A Broken Thread To A Tighter Rein	Mary Harknett	63
Family Life	Viv Eckett	64
Missing You	Justin Stonell	65
Expecting A Baby	Joy Bartelt	66
Family Ties	Jamie-Lee Johannsmann	68
Grandson	Alex Laird	69
57 Year Anniversary	Marilyn Cahane	70
Letter Writing	J Glew	71
Praise And Thanks To God For My Children	Ruth Baker	72
My Husband And I	Jeff Garland	74
Dad	Jeanette Davies	75
'Twas Ever Thus	Brian Strand	76
She Said	S Wellings	77

Absences	Norman Bissett	78
Mother Of Mine	Richard Mahoney	79
Fondest Memories	Helen Adams	80
Eleanor	Rebecca Lee	81
Family	Dalwara Singh Dulay	82
Hopes And Dreams	J E Fitzgerald	83
Saving Grace	Dianne Aspey	84
Schooldays Bell Time!	David Duthie	86
No Kid Is A Bad Kid	Margaret Wormald	89
A Daughter's Birthday	Stephen Morse	90
For Elkie	Sharon Mary Birch	91
Fragile Union	Kathleen Potter	92
Tell Me	Carmen M Pursifull & Edward L Smith	93
The Touch Of Your Hand	Freddy Gates	94
Son's Goodbye	Maria Daines	95
Your 47th Birthday	Richard Gould	96
You Are	Polly Davies	98
Bus Stop	Olive Hudson	99
A Hot Dry Summer	D Morgan	100
Late October Day	Sheila A Waterhouse	101
Lovers In Autumn	J M Armstead	102
Dahlias	Dorothy Buyers	103
September	Christina Miller	104
Season's Delight	R D Hiscoke	105
Autumn Dreams	Paula Fox	106
Every Leaf A Soul	Terry Lane	107
The Glade	Sarah Diskin	108
A Window With A View	Betty Broom	109
The Quality Of Trees	Anne Greenhow	110
Autumn	Joy Morton	111
Past Prime Of Life	David Sewell Hawkins	112
Autumn Morning	Angus Sinclair	113
Love Affair	Susan E Roffey	114

LET ME

Let me snuggle a little longer,
In the comfort of your arms.
Warm, safe, and free from danger,
Surrendering to peace and calm.

Let me look with awe and wonder,
At your body lying there.
Watch your breathing while you slumber,
Dreaming, tranquil, unaware.

Let me love you like I want to,
With my heart, and all my soul.
Passionately and unabated,
I will give to you my all.

I don't want to harm or trap you,
I will never let you down.
Find it in your heart to trust me,
Then let me love you all I can.

Sharon Spencer

YELLOW DROPS

burning drops of life
dripping off an old man's jacket
memory drops falling
from a wet grey roof
a taxi purring loudly
in the quiet road
giving a ride to antiquity
melting yellow
no parking lines
in the polluting storm
drinking in the rain
warm beer in the glass
it's just my father coming home

John Ball

TAKE ME IN YOUR ARMS

Take me in your arms
        and make me young again,
give me back the sparkle and the glow,
only you are witness to my pain,
only you would even want to know.

Take me in your arms
        and save me from my past,
give me strength to firmly close the door,
expiate the wasteful guilt at last,
help me walk into the light once more.

Take me in your arms
        and love and cherish me,
nourish both my body and my soul,
let me shed the mantel others see,
allow me to assume my rightful role.

Take me in your arms
        and let me lie there,
for we have always truly been as one,
the complex knot of life we've tied so rare,
in death it cannot ever be undone.

Angela R Davies

Lament

We always knew a place
A place where we may, one day
Recall what occurred within
That tiny moment of one instant
In once smoke filled rooms

When our world must have ended
Blown in to millions of fragments
And he so small, I let him cope
Hardly did we utter a consoling word
To glide from our tear-stained lip

Departed and antithetical
Maybe they always were

And from my mind I grasp the smell of bacon
In the kitchen
Creeping up the stairs
The pirouette of odour in the bedroom
I have forgotten of most
Of its illiberal features
The rip in the wallpaper
That captures a thousand faces

He is gone
I am still asleep to my memory
Blocked out and barred
All that lingers at the back of my mind
Recollecting shreds of idyllic song
As the lipstick smudges in the darksome room
Rhythmical on floorboards as the turntable revolves

In the park where sparrows harmoniously trill
Amidst tall trees that echo our adulthood
The sun beats down to melt our ice cream
Or orange pools that still could be tears

But we are friends
We may all lead our separate lives
Divided into quarters of what still is whole

And from afar, the train track sings
Of pastures and meadow ever green
To swell that washes over ebony pebbles
As enigmatical as his eyes
To wash away our tears

Sammy

You

You are
You say
A speck in the universe
A drop of rain
A grain of sand
To me
You are
A beach
A shower
Everything

Moira H Thorburn

BETRAYED

I thought your love was true
That you were meant for me
To live our lives together
But you betrayed my trust
And wandered to another
Without a backward glance

The hurt you did to me
I cannot explain
Some day you may find
The tables turned on you

Too late you may realise
The mistake you did make
But I won't be around
To start our life anew

Alice Higham

MY FAMILY TREASURES
(Dedicated to my my two sons Allan and David, with love Mam)

Down memory lane
I will go
To a little girl, happy and loved,
Then through the years
To a mother, nursing,
Tending her sons,
Giving the love they need.

A Grandma now
Is that young mother,
Loved, tended, cared for each day
By those who show their love.
My sons, you are my
Measures of gold.
I hold you close in my heart for ever,
My family, my golden treasures.

Jean Gill

DON'T GO

Don't let tomorrow come
Or, if it must
Let it not be true
That you will go
And I will no more see you smile
Nor hear your well-loved voice
For such a long time
It could be forever
And a chill grips my heart

I must be civilised and smile and
Say the sweet platitudes of Au Revoir.
I would shout and scream and tear my hair
But to what avail
Your life is there
Far away where I cannot reach.

Your happiness is mine,
Your sadness, my woe.
I would not keep you if I could
But oh, I wish you would not go!

G M Pilkington

ONE MORE TIME
(Dedicated to my father
Arthur Charles Pacey 1915 - 1996)

When you love someone
Never say 'Goodbye'
Always say 'I love you'
Because you never know
If that's the last time
You'll ever gaze on their face again.

That night when I left you
Ill in your hospital bed,
Family moving noisily around us,
I looked into your grey sad eyes and said
'Goodbye.'

Why that night of all nights, didn't I tell you
As I always did before I left,
'I love you?'
Did we know as I kissed you and left
That it would be the last time?

Why did you go?
You left before I said
All the things I meant to say.
Deep feelings stored in my heart but never said
I hope you knew my heart.

Will I get the chance to tell you?
Is death the end
Or just a new beginning?
When my time comes will I get one more time
To say - 'I love you Dad.'

Susan Watson

ON OUR ANNIVERSARY

I count the years I've known you,
I recall them with a smile.
Our love's so rich in happiness
So who couldn't help but
Reminisce for a while.

Our marriage has lasted
More than a day.
Yes 16 enchanting years.
So it would be hard
To take a passage of time apart
And say, yes, that was the year.

So we are full of insight
After all these joyous years.
Our love remains,
Till the Lord calls us home.
The secret of life is ours.

David A Reddish

TELL HIM ABOUT IT

His startling deep blue eyes
Looked quizzically at me
from under the blue peaked cap
His body movement languid
as he stood in front of us
Waiting to be introduced
Tropical skies and warm sensuous air
fanned the flame of love
ignited in each one
Now forty years on
the deep blue eyes
have lost their piercing gaze
The languid pose of his six foot frame
now bent and more stiffly held
The blending of two private lives
Into the ageing couple
Each content with what the other knows
A love now so deeply entwined
Even catches the other's thought
and voices it aloud
Minor irritations pass by
The rise and fall of life's event
The eternal school we both attend
Step by step and side by side
We lean inwards for support
To face the world outside

Frances Ann Hall

I'll Always Love You

When I walk past or see you there
I feel uncomfortable and as though
people have stopped to stare
To say I once felt warmth and
a part of your team
It's as though it was only part of a dream

Every time I saw you
my legs would go to jelly
I felt the butterflies
that so often flew inside my tummy

My heart would race
and I felt a longing
to be close to you
So many times the words
I'd try to say
but all the time, you were pushing me
further and further away.

Maria Jenkinson

FIRST CONCERT/FIRST LOVE

the ground shivers
with the thrum of music
and two hearts
beating alone in the crowd

his arms are wrapped around me
and his lips brush against my neck
we sway together, eyes closed against the
growing heat and darkness,

conscious only of each other
while on stage, a god like being sings
with all his soul
and

in one, shimmering moment -
love is perfect in an imperfect world
and it soars above the music,
wrapped in our kiss
as our fingertips brush heaven.

Lucy Coelho

FOR GREN

I owe to you much more than this
A hug, a smile, a tear, a kiss.
You showed me how to live again
When I said life was all in vain.
How to forgive the faults we see
In others - as you did in me,
You gave me all the love you had
To help when I was feeling sad.
You gave me hope when hope was gone
You gave me faith when I had none,
You held me close and dried my tears
Your laughter banished all my fears.
You have made my life worthwhile
Now I can face it with a smile,
I can say, because it's true
I owe my life - my dear - to you.

Lydia Barnett

THE SILENCE OF THE NIGHT

The silence of the night
    hovers over the sleeping earth.
Darkness enshrouds the heavens
    in soft swirling shadows.

In the silence of the night
    my secret dreams take wing
and I send you my angel
    to proclaim my love.

In the silence of the night
    my soul may speak to you
when no one else can hear
    the language of my love.

In the silence of the night
    I have known your soul
since time began
    and when I look into your eyes
I know I'm coming home.

Brigitta D'Arcy

Untitled
(For Stefan)

Come run with me
through the fields of my dreams

Rest a while by the cool mountain stream.

And under a diamond-filled sky
in my arms you can lie

Till the glow of morning light touches our faces

Come with me.
I will take you to many places.

Sheila Atkinson

CASTLES

You were short
and not good looking.
Your jaw, uneven, caused your chin
to jut out
giving you the appearance
of someone being led
by an invisible ring
attached to your chin.
Your eyes, protruding slightly,
gave you a glaring expression.
Walking on flat feet
which turned outwards,
you seemed like a diver,
emerging from the sea,
but we were friends.
You took me everywhere with you,
I mingled with your social circle.
And then,
you slept with me
and sent me a card saying,
you didn't know what to say,
and so, you said nothing.
From that point on
or a point somewhere just before it,
you kept me to yourself,
kept me from the others.
I, a single parent, had no one.
I thought I had a friend in you.
'I won't marry you,' you said.
You wanted to be socially acceptable.
You married a short girl,
and moved to a new town.

My baby son pulled himself upright,
holding on to a chair . . .
'Da, da, da, dada, dada, da,
dadadada, daaaa,' he said.

Linda Landers

THE BEACH
(To Julio - From Nina)

A peaceful, tranquil place.
Crumbling sandstone cliffs,
Sculptured, majestic,
In various shades of
Cream and terracotta.
Glorious pine trees, silent sentinels
Dense and protective
Like an army, arms outstretched,
Upright and strong,
Some weary and leaning,
Some fallen.
Brilliant sun
Changing the tumbling waves
Into millions of glittering gems
Blinding the unprotected eye.
Powerful watery hillocks
Crashing in a frenzy of foam
Playing an orchestral overture.
White fragile wisps of floating cloud
Against a canopy of palest blue
Like a natural movie
Bringing peace and thoughtful contemplation
Of loved ones near,
Yet very far away,
With us still,
But gone forever.

Nina Woolf

ME AND YOU

I knew straight away we'd be forever
Me and you, always together.
We fit neatly as one,
Never to be torn apart.
Whatever comes, now and then,
The past, today, is ours for the future.

Kathryn Pope

My Jim

I met him in a factory
We were in our twenties.
He had a Triumph motorbike
And went everywhere together
Then we fell in love

We married in March 1958
And had lots of laughs over the years.
We had four children,
Three girls and a son.

He is my husband and friend,
I still love him now.
My Jim has a lovely smile
And is very good to me.

We still have lots of laughs
At all the years gone by.
Those were the days.
My Jim made them great.
I thank you Jim, for everything.

Rita Johnson

YOU ARE PART OF ME

Nothing needs to be said
No great declaration of love
No grand gestures that require lavish gifts
For you are simply a part of me
We are joined by an invisible thread.

Lynda Long

CYMBELINE

The sun sets in your memory, lets the winged horse take his flight
Into the light of every dream gold seams in grey twilight
Streams of light flow through your thoughts where colours
                                                    stroke your mind
You ride on azure, ruby ports on seas of sky are lined

Those loveless lands of foreign shores in your world don't exist
With open hands through corridors of ancient realms you stroll on mist
And cross the clouds on consciousness your footsteps remain hidden
In zephyrs drunk on gentleness your secret stays forbidden

In endless forests are you lost the rivers kiss the seas
Of solace - there the bridge you crossed with whispers in the breeze
And on them are you sailing on the fate of long lost ships
The ghosts behind you trailing in the wake of full eclipse

Your life lies in the meadows where echoes hail the plains
A heaven in the shadows above the falling rains
Oh Cymbeline I taste your wine I long for your caress
Your nectar lips on honey dine I lose my senselessness

Cymbeline the world does shine inside your golden hair
Behind blue eyes a silent shrine a spirit floating in mid-air
Take me to your sanctuary the zenith of existence
To glide with you eternally on wings to bring assistance

I'll put up no resistance you touch the true sublime
Your closeness and your distance for I love you Cymbeline.

Sparky

TRUE

My love for you
Grows each day
It's larger than
Any pain
My heart pounds to
Your name.
You really are
Very special in
Every way,
I love your voice,
Your laugh, your smile
It makes my body feel like
I've been running for miles.
We are equally there for
Each other,
My darling it's you
I wish to be with and
No other.

Paula Natalie Burgess

ETERNAL EMBER

The poetry emotion
   unspoke in our time,
A transparent feeling
   read through the eyes.

B Barter

SHE IS YOU

'Who is she?' they ask.
... she is my soul's perfect mate, my body's passionate lover
and my mind's close companion.

'What is she?' they ask.
.. ... she is the rhythm of my soul, the song of my spirit
and the love of my life.

'Where is she?' they ask.
... she is in my every breath, in the beating of my heart
and in the thread that stitches my whole being together.

'When is she?' they ask.
... she is today, at dawn; tonight, when the stars come out
and tomorrow and forever.

'Why is she?' they ask.
... she is my completion, my destiny
and my spiritual complement.

'Who is she?' the ask again.
... she is you, my beloved ...
... she is you.

Ray Smith

IF A SMILE MAY TELL ME

If a wonderful life - to me be opened
If in a moment was I smitten over to her
If a smile faded; then broadened; readily to my heart beckoned
If spoke we, a little - all to me was silver and gold
If answer was made and remark told
If I liked her, was I yet to love her, how pleased was I we met
If in life to come, in an instant to look, if to shape my life,
If in her hands held she my being
If to sensuous flesh - may I be invited - so had I wanted her
If knowing her so forever shall I be contented
If I knew it all when I saw her there - may I see her more
If to share her body - may I know it well
If I found, did I not, what I was looking for - if all be all
If rest I yet upon her breasts - feel her warmth, our bodies
entwined together - shall be all I need forever and ever.

C J Bayless

NOTHING WITHOUT YOU!

Dreaming of the one person who understands,
Looking through each other's eyes,
Feeling the same emotions through each other's hearts,
You're in my heart and in my head and without you I feel so
                                    loveless and lost.

Wherever we walk, whoever we talk to,
Our steps create the same body heat,
Our mouths speak the same words,
No matter if apart, or talking to a stranger I will always miss you.

No matter what I do, or what I say!
We say everything for each other,
We do everything for each other,
No matter what I do, or what you say I will always love you.

Whatever we touch, or any other sense that we use,
The best sensation in the world is touching you,
The worst feeling of all is longing for you,
Let me grow with you, age doesn't matter, so when we're old
   and grey I'll share this with you and our children, just to show
     that 'I'm nothing without you!'

Gary Thompson

MANDY

You were called after the song of that name
The result of an illicit affair by your mother
You wanted me
And that's the reason you let me talk about my brother
It was beautiful all the same
You were the only one that got that far
And I've got Mandy on my mind.

Noel Thaddeus Lawler

AND I WILL SEE YOU IN THE MORNING

And I will see you in the morning.
And reach out to touch your face.
A halo of auburn hair surrounding you.
Lost in the luxury of the silk bedclothes
Which lap around our naked waists.
Your skin satin-smooth and pale.
The warm scent of your fragrant body I inhale.
As the morning light grows ever bright.
Golden sunbeams falling,
Upon the perfection of your face
The peach-ripe cheeks and upturned chin.
Your azure eyes, now open wide.
Twin pools, laughing; liquid cool.
Which reflectively, welcomes me, to dive in.
Those cherry-sweet lips, begging to be kissed.
Your whole demure, my perfect china doll,
My own true love, my blessed paramour.
How did a fool like myself win?
The right to hold you.
My body to enfold you.
Our two hearts, seemingly tenanted by one soul.
May angels' wings ever enfold us.
For how can one united, eager soul exist,
Beneath the duality of our two skins?

Jonathan Pegg

I LOVE YOU

'I love you',
My words descend
From the mountain peak.
'I love you', calls back,
The echoes run free.
'I love you,' I cry
As my tears gently fall
And collide with the sun,
A rainbow is formed.
'I love you,' I shout,
No anger is vented,
Just the depths of my soul,
And my heart represented.

Sue Umanski

LONELY HEART

I miss you so much when we have to part
it feels like a knife penetrating my heart.
It makes my heart die with the sorrow and pain,
and inside my heart tears drop like rain.
It cries all alone, so soft you can't hear
but deep in my eyes my love is so clear.

Put your mouth to my lips,
slide you hands around my hips.
hold me close please don't let go,
Let's make love nice and slow.
Because some love one
while others love two
but I love one and that is you.
Together forever you're engraved in my heart,
together forever we will never part.

Halima Hussain

You're Never Far Away

You're never far away
Even when I'm left alone,
For I know your face so well,
Like the pain that I have known.
Every day I see your smile,
And hear the things you say;
And because you're in my heart,
You're never far away.

I hate to see you go,
I hate to see you leave;
For I still love you so,
And this I still believe.
I can't look into your eyes
I can't bring myself to say
But no matter where you go,
You're never far away.

Even though you cannot know
Just the way I feel for you,
I still think of you each day,
And dream the whole night through.
Though you may be far from me,
Though you may not ever stay
In my mind and in my heart,
You're never far away.

David Russell

FRAGILE IS LOVE

Passion is strong while fragile is love
Ferocious is the eagle, as gentle is the dove
A love so secure can easily break
When misunderstanding, causes needless heartache

Ingrained in the heart is sincerity
But the mind sometimes wanders with infidelity
Idle rumours they plant seeds of doubt
Embroiled in suspicion, puts a loving flame out

Fragile is love treat it tenderly
Keeping no secrets, that holds the key
An open relationship forever is strong
Where friends who are lovers, will never go wrong

Samson was strong but for love became weak
Delilah deceived him for the answers she seek
Deception and heartaches we must rise above
Not for a moment forgetting, that fragile is love.

Ainsley McKenzie

QUESTIONS

Do answers exist.
Are questions - real,
or simple figments,
of humble human emotions?

While we're told one thing,
yet our hearts - feel another.
Different and so removed,
from all we see or feel.
What we hear - or believe.

What is reality,
is it truly - believable,
or is it how we feel,
or how we think it should be?

What is emotion or desire,
other than - what's simple nature.
Taking over from our ideas,
preconceived and self-destructive.

Gary J Finlay

WINTER'S REALITY

Winter arrived and seemingly crept into my life,
leaving my heart cold and forcing my memories
to wander to your doorstep.

I stand at the window and see you sitting there,
wishing that I could be next to you again,
to feel your eyes looking at me, just to feel your warmth.

To hear you speak my name, made my heart skip a beat,
a moment in time when I truly did feel complete . . . but then
reality sets in and I see my breath on frosted glass and
my dream starts melting . . .

Winter is here and you are not,
You are my summer, the one I haven't got.

Johan Botha

WE DON'T CHOOSE WE JUST FALL

Why can't we choose when we fall?
Why do we always go for the most forbidden of all?

The one who's taken, the one who's banned,
The one who sends shivers down your back,
Just by touching your hand.

The one who makes you blush when they smile,
And beam inside when they stay awhile.

The one who can just call your name,
And yet make your heart ache with pain.

The one you think of when they're not around,
The one you want to be with when no one else is around.

The one who looks amazing in whatever they wear,
The one with the perfectly styled hair.
The one that always catches your eye,
And can brighten up any sky.

The one you long to kiss and stay with all night,
The one you want to keep safe and call your own,
The one you know you can never bring home.

You know you can't have them,
And they belong to somebody other than you,
But why do we fall for them and they have such an effect on you?

They're the wrong one who loves you right,
And keeps you up thinking all night.

I know we can't choose when we fall,
But why do we always seem to fall for the most forbidden of all?

This is just nature and the answer we'll never know,
But how will the story end for each of us though?

Will we get one moment of lust, one night of love,
Or turned away to dusk?
We don't choose, we just fall . . .

And I've fallen for you.

Lynsey Tocker

QUESTIONS

Her tears can fill a river,
dark circles under here eyes,
sobs of sorrow fill the air,
raised question, why!
Fairness is all she asks,
his arms she longs for,
his kisses her mouth waits for,
his touch, his taut body,
to hold him, his name revolves
around her head every waking time,
she is proud of her man,
her precious *soldier* man!
Time apart so bad, phone calls,
red-hot lines,
photos smile at every angle,
taken in Paris *on parade*
love surrounds her,
she must share her man,
never for a moment
let him know how it hurts,
she waits, smiles for him,
love him, just love him.

Wendy-Elezabeth

MARRIAGE

She
loved him
for saving her from
a turbulent passage
across the open sea.
He
loved her
because she gave him
peace
and a chance to
sail in the sun again.
I think that's why
they're able to weather storms
so much
and to keep their
ship from sinking.

Trisha Matthews

UNTITLED

Many times I've seen your face,
In the dreams of regret and pain.
Emotion,
Like the tide,
In, out,
Out, in.
Wear away the sands of time.
The sun is beating,
It's winter in my heart.
Cold and harassed,
Frightened and confused.
Do I dare to call your name?

A sudden insight,
There's light up ahead.
A glorious sense of being I feel.
Like a phoenix from the ashes,
My heart melted into spring.
Love, warmth,
Strength to let go.
The present and future are all that matter,
Now I see love from every angle.

Donna Salisbury

VICTORIA

Across a field of daffodils, a young bonnie lassie walked,
The air was filled with music, as that bonnie lassie talked,
Her golden hair was flowing, in a soft but gentle breeze,
Victoria, Victoria, there's many the hearts you'll please.

My bonnie lass I love you so, with a smile to melt one's heart,
Oh bonnie lass for one so young, you're many miles apart,
From all those lovely rivals, you'll meet along the way,
Victoria, sweet Victoria, it's my number one you'll stay.

My bonnie lass when you are near, a tear forms in my eyes,
Like a little angel on a cloud, you're a cherub from the sky,
Your lovely eyes are twinkling, so bright but yet serene,
Victoria, sweet Victoria, you compare with a lovely dream.

I've treasured all the things we've done, with memories galore,
Those lovely hours I've spent, with the baby that I adore,
Victoria, sweet Victoria, named after a famous Queen,
Victoria, dear Victoria, you're the loveliest baby I've seen.

Sandy Laird

YESTERDAY
(Written on May 10th 1999, the day following the memorial walk in Ystradfellte organised by the National Park in memory of David)

Yesterday
We walked in your footsteps,
Traced the paths you loved to tread,
Ploughed through nettles and mud,
Drank in the perfume of trees and wild flowers,
Marvelled at the torrent of tumbling falls,
Shed the encumbrances of civilisation
So that we were at one with nature
As you were every wondrous working day.

Yesterday
As on other occasions since your death,
I was humbled to learn
How little I knew of the man I had married
Four decades earlier.
I learned of your other life,
The life of the true and real you.
The event itself witnessed your colleagues' high esteem of you.
All extolled your virtues,
Regaled me with tales of incidents
Characteristic of the essence of you.

And yesterday,
As I stood by the unfinished wall
Supported by makeshift wooden posts
Surrounded by the stones
You had selected
To complete your final task,
My soul soared to meet you
And we were united more completely
Than we ever had been in life.

In those brief moments
The full awareness of the extent of my loss
Flooded in on me,
Drowning my will to live,
Overwhelming me with the desire
To renounce this world
For spiritual oneness with you.

Marian Morgan

A Poem For My Mum
(I would like to dedicate this poem to my mother, who had an unexpected lumpectomy in 2001)

How could it have happened?
We were so careful with you little one:
A cold,
Or perhaps too much sun -
You hear of that!

Nicola Barnes

MY DAD

His voice was soft
He never raised his hand
To us kids
I remember the way
He stood with his hands in his pockets
Jingling his loose change
He was always smart
Shining the shoes was a must
In our house.
He loved sport
The badminton rackets
Had their place on the top of the wardrobe
Football and cricket in their alternate seasons
And when we got our first television
He never missed a match.
I miss my dad
He died thirty-two years ago
But I'm still his little girl in my heart.

Moira Clelland

MY SON STEVEN

Looking for you all the time
The days we would have had
Are gone, why did you
Have to go? It seems endless
Like the sun. As you were
Taken away from me.
My thoughts are just
For you. When a new day
Dawns it holds no pleasure
For me. But the shadows
Darken to end of the day
I love you to the end of time.

R E Bilson

THE GENTLEMAN PUGILIST

He is a gentle man and confidant,
So kind and full of heart.
Humble and a Trojan
And the master of his art.
Our town supports him all the way
His name we speak with pride;
The young ones all look up to him
His fans come far and wide.
He sports a dedication
Only found in those who stay
To be the best and teach the rest
The skill shown on display.
To see him fight is poetry
In motion. Not a brawl,
For as it stands, his art commands
It's all about control.
So proud am I to know this guy
As so are many more;
The one and only Tony Byrne
Is Preston's own hero.

Linda Zulaica

TO KATE

As you lie beside me, your love flows into me like a flood
- like a flood bringing life to meadows.
The flood recedes and cowslips spring, and horses feed
On the rich banks, their coats shining in the sun.
Your love is permanent as the mountains
That appear serene through mist,
That are clothed in snow by winter,
That rejoice in the sun of summer,
Yet never change.
So unending is your love.

Angus Sinclair

TO MY MOTHER

We shall not pass this way again:
An easy thought, not new,
Often said, no less true.

Familiar gesture, smile, turn of phrase:
Easy, thoughtless, not meant
To last but in the end

Is what remains, indelibly:
In actions and in mind
Those mem'ries, intertwin'd,

Are what I am. Or rather, then
And now are added to
Myself, make something new.

Alan Wooding

LABOUR OF LOVE

Two become one
In passionate embrace.
Planting seeds,
New life conceived.
Since Adam and Eve
Tasted the first fruit
Of the forbidden tree,
Human form began.
A nine month bond
Linking mother with child.
Man, born of woman,
Helpless, looking on.
Witness to a labour of love.
There is nothing quite like
Sharing a bundle of wonder.

Phil Clayton

MOTHER/DAUGHTER, THE RELATIONSHIP OR BRIDGE THAT GAP

Then - a long void going nowhere.
Two entities walking on in their own spheres
Without a meeting point -
That was how it was.

Now - over time a bridge has been constructed,
New eyes view each other over the gap.
The bond is there. The spell is broken.
Truth, love, understanding and compassion
Weld themselves into an indestructible, beautiful structure,
Which, like the *Millennium Bridge*, will,
Despite the previous *wobbles*,
Stand forever - a monument in time.

M Fitzpatrick Jones

FAMILY TIES

Unspoken words
A mutual love
The fact you stayed was proof

Companionship
A loyalty
Even though at times aloof

Calming skills
With languid style
Your precious time to give

Wild antics,
Playful, happiness
The memories still live

We shared a life
Telepathy
We mixed and matched together

Worries shared
A confidante
But stand in judgement? Never!

Thankful, grateful
Listening friend
The tears once more are flowing

Not just a cat
Much more than that
The thoughts of you, still growing.

Kay Astbury

THANK YOU MY SPIRIT CHILD

It's been a long while now
When your seed was planted - a divine gift
In my womb I carried you
My lifeline was your lifeline, we shared everything
Together we received nature's abundance
Our love, our feelings, our thoughts, our beings
All in harmony.

Your first touch, caressing and reassuring
As if to say, 'Hi there, I know you know who I am
I am your spirit child and I know who you are my co-creator'
I, co-creator? - I marvelled.

It's been a long while now
When you made your debut one fine morning
You arrived strong and vibrant
Your first respire, your initiation into this earthly plane
Witnessed by the highest order, seen and unseen

It's been a long while now
When you cried, my spirit awakened
I held you close to my heart when you suckled
Our heartbeats synchronised
Without a word we understood each other

It's been a long while now
Your brown eyes beholding inner peace and love
Your smile, a tonic to the soul
Your delicate hands, healing received
Your first steps - tiny steps, giant leap to greatness
Your quest for knowledge, your desire for freedom unabated

It's been a long while now
A beautiful, unique child you have been
Your mission, a choice for you to make
Walking your path in life

It's been a long while now
The web of life's great expectations
Marked trials and challenges of co-existence
Yet, no judgement but gratitude
As we were bound together in love and in strength
Our lives flowing in abundance and more
Every moment precious
Every moment treasured
Every moment sacred

It's been a long while now
You knew me before the dawn of the day
You chose me to be your eternal mother
You honoured my being
Elevated me above the ordinary
Thank you my spiritual child.

Meg Aku Sika Millar

THANK YOU DAD

Thank you for your affection and protection,
Thank you for your hard work and sincerity,
You will always
Be a special person to me.

I love you dear dad,
Sorry for the times I was a pain,
My love for you,
Will always remain.

Thank you for your concern,
Thank you for your caring,
When I was in the wrong,
Thank you for your guiding.

Let's forget any bad times,
Remember the good,
I will always love you,
Let it be understood.

You are always there for me,
And it's nice to know,
That if I am in trouble,
You will help me so.

When your days on Earth are over, dear dad,
You will go to Heaven up above,
Take with you dear father,
My endless love.

I will join you in Heaven,
It's good to know,
We will be happy and content,
My love for you will continue to grow.

We are born,
We live, we love and we die,
While we are on this Earth,
Let's be happy and continue
When we meet again
In Heaven up in the sky.

John Lewis

AMMÂH ENNAIRAM
(Dedicated to my mother)

A godly mother; hard to find
A mother with treasures; yet unearthed
Past compare; nature's love
'Stablished by divine hands
A godly mother; hard to find.

A godly mother; yet mine
Raised to mould
Furnished in nature's womb
Beauty past compare; hard to find
Bursts of praise; all around; a godly mother; hard to find.

A godly mother; ennairam
Deposits of gold; hidden glistens from depths within,
Eyes feathered lightly
Lines; roundabout of wisdom
Nature's very craft; mother such like;
Hard to find.

A godly mother; the form of comfort embodied
Hands lifted to God; interceding for all
Bringing change to the world around
Surrounded by the very presence of God
Nature's very craft; peace to the soul; hard to find; a mother such like.

From the bosom of God;
Brought forth unto the;
Shores of Earth; see and smile in agreement to;
Satisfying divine heartbeats
Depositing of her life without
A godly mother; ours, past compare.

Patricia Aboagye

GRAN

Warm and plump,
With a lap,
As cosy as a feathered nest.
Hair, white and wavy,
And skin warm and mellow,
She smiles,
Offering eggs for breakfast,
Frying each one with care
Flicking sizzling fat over,
To cook the yolks to perfection,
Stomachs full and content,
Off to the beach,
Where she watches and laughs,
While we dig the sand,
And are chased,
By the incoming tide.

Later gathered around a feast,
Lemon curd pie,
Crumbling pastry, sweet and tart,
Cakes, sandwiches, cheese.
Satiated and glowing we are,
Sleepily tucked in crisp sheets,
By hands so kind and loving.
Her life entwined with ours,
Like an eternal embrace.

N Lord

MY FATHER

I think of how you stood for hours
Making wonderful things;
Radios, cameras, clocks and machines
From bits and pieces in rusty tins,
My father.

I never knew what you really thought
About so many things,
Or why you never spoke of life -
Your memories or feelings,
My father.

What was your life inside your head?
Why was nothing shared?
Too much buried, unexplained,
Under obligation?
My father.

You could have done exciting things,
Used talents in the war,
Inventions and experiments
Instead of daily chore,
My father.

What dreams did you surrender?
What chances slipped away
Because you wouldn't leave us,
Honour-bound to stay?
My father.

I wish I could have known you
As you really were,
And found the ground between us
In the life we shared,
My father.

Jane Ward

FROM A BROKEN THREAD TO A TIGHTER REIN

I used to hear
Your ev'ry breath.
I used to feel
Your pain.
I used to sense
When you were close
And how to make you smile.
But now
The hours
Of time
Have passed,
Like miles
Between
And
Through -
That then was then
And now is now
And truly
I hardly
Knew
You.

Mary Harknett

FAMILY LIFE

When will they give me peace and quiet my mind cries out
to me.
If it's not the telly blaring out, it's their crazy music
pounding loudly.

Then their dad comes home from work 'Oi! You two keep
the noise down.' he shouts at the top of his voice.

Someone's knocking at the door.
The dogs start barking madly, the parrot squawking too.
'Anyone gonna answer that bloody door?' hubby yells out
angrily. Meaning me!

Oh just to sit and daydream or
To wander around the garden without the kids shouting,
'Mum have you washed my white shirt? What's for dinner tonight?
You know I don't like faggots!'
'I can't find my maths book. He's calling me names again Mum.'
'No I'm not, if you grass on me again I'll smash your face in.'

Then I yell, 'I've had just about enough of you two!'
'Oh chill out Mum, don't get in a stress.'
'Give us a break Mum.'

Then my hubby, bless his heart!
Turns to me and says, 'You look exhausted love, why don't you
finish up those dishes and make a nice cup of tea, then come
and have a rest.'

'Oh by the way, before you do there's something I must tell you,
We're overdrawn at the bank; our cheques are bouncing too.
But don't you worry love, you just come and put your feet up
And have a nice cuppa with me.'

Viv Eckett

MISSING YOU

Lately, I've been working by the sea.
Alongside me, my workmate Toby.
Even when working it's a nice place to be.
I just wish I wasn't, and my family were here with me.
I miss my girls and my beautiful wife;
I find it so frustrating, this working life.
I know most of the responsibility to provide is mine;
I just wish I could give my family more of my time.
I don't see my girls getting up in the morning,
stomping around, tired-eyed and yawning.
Going downstairs to find some food,
then kids' TV to lighten their mood.
Back upstairs to wake Mum from the dead,
pulling and shouting until she rolls out of bed.
Mum accepting that it's no longer night but day.
School, shopping, work and all those bills to pay.
It can't be easy all the roles she has to perform,
and for the millions of others for which it's the norm.
My love for her is so true, faithful and sincere,
I feel as if I'm missing a limb when she's not near.
Don't get me wrong, we argue and fight,
the kids being naughty and money being tight.
But we have something so secure and stable,
I don't think divorce papers will ever be on the table.
And then there's the love for my little ladies,
they've changed my life ever since they were babies.
They're so often naughty and so rarely good,
but if I had to give my life for them I would.
So people that say winning the lottery can be a problem,
they must be mad, I'd take the money straight off them.
I'd be over the moon and spend it as I should,
and be with my loved ones every moment I could.

Justin Stonell

EXPECTING A BABY

Been a lovely pregnancy.
Enjoyed every moment of it
Watched the baby grow
Wonder above wonders.
It kicked one day,
A footballer in the making.
One day we named her.
Emma, a strong name.
What a pretty picture on the scan.
Eating for two now, what fun.
Not drinking alcohol or smoking.
Being very careful.
Don't want to take any risks
Carrying a precious bundle.
Doctor keeping a careful eye on me.
Doing my exercises ready for the birth.
Gone into labour.
Waters broke.
Off to hospital.
Gown on
Beginning to feel the pains.
Do the breathing exercises.
God, that was a bad one.
Clinging onto the bedhead.
The midwives are giving me something to help.
Push again, do as they say.
God, is it going on for ever?
The sweat is pouring off me
I will give one gigantic scream,
Perhaps that will help.
God, it didn't.

I cry out for something more for the pain
Someone shouts 'It's coming.'
The head has appeared.
One last heave!
The baby is out.
Into my arms.
Ten perfect fingers,
Ten perfect toes.
She looks like me,
Blue eyes and blonde hair.
Even her lips and nose are mine.
She lies there so quiet and still, bless her.
She is going to be such a good girl.
What is that they're saying?
'Stillborn.'

Joy Bartelt

Family Ties

My great grandma's name was Mary,
although she was nicknamed Doe.
She seems the kind of lady
I would like to know.

She died three months before I was born,
a stubborn lady I am told.
My family sometimes say I'm Doe reincarnated.
I suppose it could be true!

She knitted a shawl before I was born
I have it to this day, to keep me safe and warm.
Every stitch she made was perfect,
For the bundle she wouldn't see.

Twelve years on as I snuggle it close
I knew all her love was for me.
She insisted I was to be a girl as she became very frail,
When she put her hand on Mummy's tummy I kicked her without fail.

We moved house not long ago, there were boxes by the score.
The memories those boxes held seemed to open up a door.
Of times gone by.

I have a gift, a singing voice, it's something that I treasure.
I wonder if Doe can hear it, sharing in all our pleasure?

I feel I really know this great grandma of mine,
She's had a guiding influence, with the passage of time.
She didn't need to be alive, I've known right from the start.
She is hiding somewhere . . . is it within my heart?

Jamie-Lee Johannsmann (12)

GRANDSON

You are ebbing away from me,
I feel the stretch
Each contraction brings.

You search to find your space,
That distant look, a face maturing
Denying the kisses, the warm embrace.

Words are now used like building blocks
To fill the space once filled
By grace and innocence.

Horizontals and perpendiculars
Must be set in good;
No false angles to be misread
Or misunderstood.

Alex Laird

57 Year Anniversary

My parents dear, you have been of great support to me
And I wish to express some words of thanks on this your anniversary.
I know there have been times of stress,
times when maybe I have not done my best,
but your love has never failed.
My love for you has not always come through,
but the strength to survive, through you, has prevailed.
I wish I could convey how much it means
to have a mum and dad like you both.
And though I've created some dramatic scenes,
I worked really hard at life (though some scoff).
I have in me great kindness of spirit,
and sometimes that has been my downfall.
I've cherished your words and your visits
when life has been lonely and cruel.
I have a peace now more often,
thank you for your love and support.
I wish the bad times I could soften,
and pressure I'd given you been less fraught.
But thank you for being there for me,
I hope I can be there for you.
You've made for us a strong family
in every act, wish and deed that you do.
Your love for each other is exclusive,
a hard act to follow that's for sure,
and although for me it has always been elusive,
I think I have it now, for this man's love is pure.

Marilyn Cahane

LETTER WRITING

Over the years of marriage our letters
Dear Mother were as dear to me
As our friendship. Secrets conveyed
In words travelled the miles
Sometimes filled the gap at
Times of joy and great sadness
Now I must give this joy
Of letters passed between us and my
Dear daughter to fill the miles apart
So a friendship already becomes
Strengthened and shared.

J Glew

PRAISE AND THANKS TO GOD FOR MY CHILDREN

I have so much to thank God for, in the gift of three lovely children,
And seven grandchildren. I give thanks every day.
But most of all I thank Him for my eldest daughter Beryl.

I had a difficult time just over 50 years ago,
When I was working as a district midwife and she was about to be born.
A long and painful delivery, but praise God He brought me through.

Now at 83, disabled and widowed, I praise God for Beryl,
Who, though very busy with family of her own,
students and a large house,
She finds time to help me so much.

I am grateful to God for all my children, they all do things
for me at times,
But Beryl, living nearer, does my shopping, which I am
no longer able to do,
Takes me out at times to the doctors, to the hospital and other places,
Sometimes taking me to her home for a lovely meal.

Helen her daughter, married to a lovely Christian,
Also helps her, sometimes taking me out and also helping
in other ways.
Another lovely Christian is my adopted granddaughter
over the Pennines,
She is also very good to me in different ways, together with her friend.

Sylvia my younger daughter takes me to her home once a month,
And visits me each week, but she is not married and has a full-time job.
Ray my son and his family have taken me on holidays on the
Canals several times and fetched me over the Pennines to stay
with them now and again.
They have two adopted little boys with Down's Syndrome
Besides two boys of their own.

So you see I have much to praise and thank God for always,
All these blessings He has given to me. Such a lovely helpful family.
I praise Him also, that they all love the Lord Jesus,
And seek to serve Him, as I do also, in my daily life.

Ruth Baker

MY HUSBAND AND I

Glazed street terracing at the Burlington
Hotel shades a lone couple. Unseasonal
the weather, even for Eastbourne, you'd agree:
mid-day November sunshine, calligraphy
by Dufy, a scrawled postcard fresh from Heaven.

Arranged and framed in Lloyd Loom chairs across
distance and stillness, they are a long-term pair.
He is jack-knifed in old man's doze; arms dangle
to the ground; his cardigan concertinas
a lullaby; pate shines soft as bedside light.

She is a stiff-backed monarch with permed crown
unwavering, upswept spectacles glinting
on a glare. Proclaimed, her consort's negligence:
we did not reckon on eternal bliss. And yet,
after so many years, how has it come to this?

Jeff Garland

Dad

Whenever I float
on my back
toes pointing skyward
quite motionless
I think of him

He tried to teach me
many things
like how to drive
and sums
not to wear make-up
or buy red boots
how to budget
not to marry young

but this floating
business
we got
spot on.

Jeanette Davies

'TWAS EVER THUS

our young carry no baggage
as mother's place is in the wrong!

careless cheery easy going
empirical experience of life
unwelcome unwanted ignored
for mother's place is in the wrong!

laid-back light-hearted
without a care
wait . . .
when trouble torments
scandal stains and shame
who's to blame?
no problem . . .
mother's place is in the wrong!

an easy target
makes no fuss!

our young carry no baggage
'twas ever thus!

Brian Strand

SHE SAID

Your heart has the look of the Marie Celeste
And Darwin's theories in your case were just a guess,
26 before your mother let you take off your vest.

He said
A huge IQ, perhaps pre-lobotomy
Costs more than a pound to enter your lottery.
You'd test even Ghandi with your inane cacophony.

She said
You always boasted you were blessed,
So why the pain behind my eyes when I see you undressed,
My vows were made under duress.

He said
If you'd only mentioned your problems with monogamy
I could have been saved all these years of agony
Your lawyer should wear an eye patch for his legalised piracy.

They said
We have to be friends for the sake of the children
Shuttled back and forth, maintain the illusion
Swallow our feelings to allay their confusion.

The children said,
What is all this, why the pain?
If this is love, we're not playing that game
Who cares who's to blame
Just hope it's not us, quick upstairs they're at it again.

S Wellings

ABSENCES
(Why did you leave? Why did you have to go,
before we'd had a chance to have a word with you?)

Eric, if you were here today, here in this room,
I would apologise, and beg your pardon for my blithe
Assumption that you'd always be around.
All through our boyhood years, you were around,
Touch judge and scorer, the eternal secretary.
I'd ask about the unspoken, the unspeakable,
And query how things were, before you went.
Also apologise, with all my heart, for thoughtlessly
Parading so much happiness before you left,
For being able to recall only the years of laughter.

Nancy, if you were here today, here in this room,
I would apologise for our unseemly optimism
Before you left, before you went away
Into the heedless night. I'd beg your pardon
For misconstruing the nature of 'new lease of life'.
I'd conjure reminiscences of Tiree
And talk about the Lebanon, Jerusalem and Pentland
Walks, about our sadness that you did not come
To Spain, Egypt and the Orient. Lost opportunities,
For which we'll tend the pansies, rue and rosemary.

And Fergie, if you were here today, here in this room,
I would apologise for getting back too late
From Nowheresville, and beg your pardon
For taking suffering as read, your remarkable
Resilience on trust. I'd thank you properly
For fifty years of friendship close to brotherhood -
Decades of kindness, worn like a second skin. I'd give
You two good reasons why we wanted to come home again.
We'd take her hand, and yours, in ours, and say, 'Goodbye,
Old friend. We'll tend the flame, until we meet again.'

Norman Bissett

MOTHER OF MINE

Oh Mother why did you walk out
And leave me here alone in a cloud?
Did you get lost in a storm or
Carried away in a crowd?
Life is so lonely here without you.
The long days and nights seem the same.
I am always thinking of you
And I don't even know your name.

Oh Mother where are you now?
Did you weather the storm?
Did you bypass the crowd
Then reach out your arms and touch me?
Take me away from my cloud.
Then the long days and nights will be over.
The long wait will not be in vain.
It will be a moment to treasure
When I hear you whisper your name.
Then I can give you some flowers.
A special spring bouquet
Made up of buttercups and daisies
When they grow again in May.
Oh Mother of mine.

Richard Mahoney

FONDEST MEMORIES
(For Nanette Sylvia Neal)

Never Grandma or even Gran,
always special Nan,
that's how the song sang.
I love your wrinkles and even your spots!
Marmite on toast,
and tea in a cup.
Never a cross word,
always a smile.
Dried onions,
not fresh,
they last a long while.
Jokes at midnight,
and card games we'd play.
The 'Grannies' Grotto' made me laugh all day.
So many memories,
too many to write down.
Feeling so lost now,
you aren't around.
Smiling at the past,
looking to the future,
I thank you Nan,
for being my teacher.

Helen Adams

ELEANOR

With purple boots
And lilac skirt
And grazes on her knees,
She jumps around
In a secret world
And gathers up the leaves,
Not that they have fallen
Or are where they should not be,
But simply so
She can hold them close
And bring them all to me.

Rebecca Lee

POEM TO BILL ON OUR 10TH WEDDING ANNIVERSARY, 18 MAY 1963

I can't believe it's only ten
There's our Philip, Jane and Pen
House and garden (running wild)
And my temper, far from mild.

What burdens those few years have heaped
Upon your head . . .
May I say 'Rewards you've reaped'
Instead?

Meg Stephenson

HOPES AND DREAMS
(Dedicated to my six children, 11 grandchildren and 3 great grandchildren)

My hopes and reams I pass on to you
My tears will be the falling rain
My kisses will touch your face
When the sun rises.
My arms will be a breeze
Blowing all around you
All the moon will guide you on your way
The stars will twinkle with the laughs we had
I love you all so much
The best kids a mum can have.

J E Fitzgerald

SAVING GRACE

Picture the scene, in the dentist chair
Bracing myself against any eventuality
Totally aware of my vulnerability
My soul unwittingly bared to the outside world.
As the dentist wrenches and looks around
At the roots of a tooth which has served me well
For years, I think of the stark brutality
Of life and the incessant decay
When out of the blue springs an old adage
'If thine eye offend thee, pluck it out!'
The stark finality of such an exhortation
Gives me something concrete to cling to
And I am inadvertently plunged headlong
Into a sea of memories.
My grandfather - who lost his eye
Through glaucoma
My dad's inherent warning,
'I always had long roots'
Set alongside the knowledge
That our teeth are so identical.
At which point, the tooth
Makes a sickening crunch
And the dentist pauses, for a break.
To cushion myself from the barbarity
Of it all, I think of how Mum
Keeps all her teeth as trophies
In her jewellery box.
This thought helps me transcend reality
Through the all enduring power of love
And the little anecdotes
Which have been programmed into us
By our forefathers to counteract
The trials and tribulations.

In times of crisis, the infinitesimal bond
Between ourselves and our forefathers
Slips into gear, strengthens our resolve
And helps us sail through.
Love is the answer.

Dianne Aspey

SCHOOLDAYS BELL TIME!

Up at eight
Wash your face
Clean your teeth
Straighten your tie
Tuck your shirt in
Make sure your smart
Mum!
Where's my PE gear?
Bus fare
Walk to school
Save money for sweets
Call for a mate
Must run
Can't be late

Bell time!
Registration
Here Sir!
Morning assembly
Head for classes
Don't run!
Wish it were playtime
And I was out in the sun

Two lessons of maths
With Mr Gittins
Adding, subtracting
Multiplication, long division
Algebra!

Bell time!
Milk time!
Play time!
Tuck shop
Run wild
Fall over
Cry baby!

Bell time!
French
With Mrs Perkins
Two merits
For reciting, 'Frere re Jacque'

Bell time!
You boy!
You know not to run
See me, in my class at lunchtime!
Music
With Mr Blake
Put-your-face-in-a-space!
Every-good-boy-deserves-favour!

Bell time!
Dinner time
Free school meals
Fish, chips and peas
Spotted dick and lumpy custard
Reported to Mr Mason
Fifty lines!
I must not run along the corridors
I must not run along the corridors
Etc, etc, etc!
Played chess, till -

Bell time!
History
With Mr Skipper
When was 'The Battle of Hastings?'
Ten sixty-six Sir!
That's history!

Bell time!
Geography
With Mr Williamson
Where's Spain?
Page twenty in the atlas!
Traced map
Coloured it

Bell time!
Playtime
Fag in toilets

Bell time!
Two lessons of English
With Mr Nutall
A drama, reading plays
Threading words together
Like diamonds on a chain
That's poetry!

Bell time!
Home time!
Fight on the playing field
Run all the way home
Hair a mess
Scuffed shoes
Tie undone
Dirty collar
Shirt hanging out
Throw down homework
Fall into the chair
Television on

Mum!
Where's my tea?

David Duthie

No Kid Is A Bad Kid

Plant seeds of encouragement, love
Support and positive attitude.
As the seed grows so does the child,
Learning, listening, growing up
With what has been planted.
Choose the seeds of love, understanding
And encouragement grows a child
With happiness and contentment.
When in full bloom creates a happy, healthy
Future so much to be proud of.
Please plant the seeds of success.

Margaret Wormald

A Daughter's Birthday

Having a daughter is a delight
Quite different from possessing boisterous boys;
She gives a sense to me of self-fulfilment,
Coming into my life like a gift -
Not me to her, but her to me.
Her birthday, thus, brings happy returns to me,
And all I have to give is love and pride.

Stephen Morse

FOR ELKIE
(My daughter and friend)

There have been times when I failed to speak,
Have forgotten to tell you how precious you are
And as you grow older, and wiser than me
I feel those omissions; I feel such a fear.

For so many years my emotions were drained
Fixing, arranging and looking elsewhere
Did I take you for granted? If so I am shamed
But always I loved you and always I care.

I look at you now and feel immense pride -
Your gentle acceptance of all that I've been
Warming my heart whilst in you I confide.
Life without you would be empty and bleak.

So know how I love you when I fail to speak
See in my eyes all the warmth I hold there
From mother to mother know my heart ever seeks
To keep you from harm and protect you from care.

And in times of sadness I feel your love
It lifts me and holds me and keeps back the night
So don't shed a tear, nor worry, my love
If you hold my hand then my world is all right.

Sharon Mary Birch

FRAGILE UNION

Wee damaged bird incapable of flight
    wings clipped by life's callous cruelty and strife.
Timid moth enmeshed in web of his light
    fearing, yet veering towards bright new life.
Caught safe in the silver web of his love,
    succour he offers; calm peace of a dove.
Such chemistry, an everlasting scroll
    written in the stars, binds soul unto soul.
As ivy clings, the trunk its pinion
    to flourish in tender stable union.
The source of life, were it ever vanquished
    fragile heart would languish impoverished.

Kathleen Potter

TELL ME

Tell me -
have you known emotion
the kind that crawls
within your thoughts
& creates havoc -
images not really known
but imagined?

Tell me -
is the wizened seer
seeing what only exists
in your imagination
or does he create
these knitted fabrics by design?

Tell me -
your needs
to feel the comforts of my love.
I am curious yet wonderless
but one thought breaks through
like a high wave for the surfer -
you have to know precisely
when to take the plunge.

Carmen M Pursifull & Edward L Smith

THE TOUCH OF YOUR HAND

The touch of your hand - makes my heart miss a beat
  Turns my head around sweeps me off my feet
Days run through my fingers just like grains of sand
  But you make time stand still with the touch of your hand.

Just the touch of your hand as it slips in mine
  And the touch of your skin as our fingers entwine
I've never felt like this and I don't understand
  The magic you weave with the touch of your hand.

Electricity flows and sparks seem to fly
  From my head to my toes as I look in your eyes
So come walk with me on the edge of the sand
  You can calm the rough sea with the touch of your hand.

I'll still feel the touch of your hand in mine
  At the end of the road at the end of my time
For whatever I've done and whatever I've planned
  I know I've been blessed by the touch of your hand.

Freddy Gates

SON'S GOODBYE

Last final stint of all your cares, go taken fondly from my arms,
like puppies grown to leggy yap, and therefore needless snuggles try,
you catch my eye, I must look up, and see the man who breaks the tie.
The saddest day to hold me tight, let go in one swift leave of hand,
from boots no bigger than a smile, your marching twelves
stride forth to plans. And mother strings now flap around,
without the work that these things do, time is left to say aloud,
for what am I? if not for you. And be you tall, convincing so,
much that others would believe, there still, inside, as I shall know,
a tiny boy who worries me. Yet all along, I knew this day,
was coming faster than I cared, just out of reach, you stepped ahead,
and made small disconnections there. A goodbye kiss, an empty room,
some solitude I hadn't seen, simple loosening of thread,
which showed through my dependency, on being someone to be free,
that, and all the other gifts, I have to say, you looked to me,
and now I have to let it be. To watch you Son, now you are grown,
would not be right to hold you back, but always, in the life you know,
a mother has a canny knack, of being where she ought to be,
when feelings of her children hurt, and you must go into the world,
and I must stay behind and catch, the golden moments, floating by,
the sadness, though so hard to watch, and all the wonder in between,
the love that makes a mother cry.

Maria Daines

YOUR 47TH BIRTHDAY

Your 47th birthday,
And you steal into my dreams,
Your 47th birthday,
And you sail across my view,
Your 47th birthday,
Still you know just how much you mean,
Your 47th birthday.

Your 47th birthday,
To me, you remain ageless,
To me, you're still the same,
How long this candle?
How strong this flame?

Your 47th birthday,
As this world teeters on the brink,
You'll be washing dishes at the sink,
Was this what any of us intended?
Were we not worthy of something better?

Your 47th birthday,
Dare we cling to our memories?
Dare we both recollect?
Dare we be once again young?
Dare we confess before the sun?

Your 47th birthday,
I wish you well and all that you desire,
May it come before the fall of night,
May you always know and feel,
That, for you, love is true and real.

Your 47th birthday,
We embraced on the other side of night,
And talked of all that goes on in our lives.
May we always be this close - if only for a while,
May we always retain the gift to each other of a smile.

Your 47th birthday
And you steal into my dreams,
Your 47th birthday,
Be gone, for now, the dawn approaches
Another tomorrow arrives for us both.

Richard Gould

YOU ARE

You are,
White kittens on black satin
Dolphins dancing on the sea
Eagles soaring the heavens
Puppies with cold noses
Black stallions racing the wind
Stags in dappled morning light
Bunnies at Easter

You are,
Yellow daffodils in green grass
Purple iris in a crystal vase
Lavender on a pillow
Snow on a far away mountain
Rain in the desert
Fresh air on a mountain's top
Blue sky within black clouds

You are,
Sunshine on a winter's day
Holding hands in public
Green palms against an orange sky
Strawberries and ice cream
Pink-tinged sunsets
Red wine and chocolates
Soft nights and music

You are -
> *Love*

Will you be my Valentine?

Polly Davies

BUS STOP

Remember the day we met at the bus stop,
Two cocky kids, and followers of fashion.
Hair a foot high, a bouffant you know,
Lashes so long I could hardly see through them,
Lips oh so shapely, painted so perfect,
Heels were so high, I nearly fell off them,
Coat the colour of gun metal, that swaggered and swayed,
As I made my move on you.
Remember that day we met at the bus stop,
Your hair was like Elvis, suit full of fashion,
Black patent shoes, socks just to match them,
We've come a long way since we met at that bus stop,
Now forty years on and everything's fading,
But still madly in love with this man at the bus stop.

Olive Hudson

FAMILY

Family, family, family,
Where would we be without our family?

Family, family, family,
How sweet my brother and sisters can be.

Sometimes we laugh, sometimes we cry,
But we always have a good fight.

My sisters are sweet and kind
And have a loving state of mind.

My brother shows me he's hard,
But I know he's soft on the inside.

My wife is kind and loving and always backs me in a fight,
Although she is only five foot five.

My kids are sweet and cute, like sugar wouldn't melt,
But deep down below there's a monster running around.

Mum and Dad are old to see,
But they always have a loving word for me.

But I myself have a dream,
That my family will live in peace.

Dalwara Singh Dulay

A Hot Dry Summer

The ground was hot and dusty
No puddles in the lane
Trees lifted up their leafy boughs
As if they prayed for rain.
Arid lawn was trying hard
Some greenness to maintain
Begging in its simple way
For cool refreshing rain.

Sagging flowers tried to lift
Their dropping heads - in vain,
How much stronger they'd have been
With the blessing of some rain.
The shrinking pond was struggling
Some water to retain
Frogs and toads were anxious for
The pit-a-pat of rain!

Cool of evening helped of course
To ease the searing pain
Of fearsome heat and dryness
Caused by the lack of rain.
But now the drought is over
And the Heavens have opened again.
My eyes are seeing the most glorious of sights
A garden in the rain!

D Morgan

LATE OCTOBER DAY

Cool crisp air of,
Early morning light.
Gossamer mists over
Meadows creep.
Sun's mellow rays burst through,
Dappled leaves fall,
As carpets deep.
Pumpkin lanterns of Hallowe'en
Tall black hats and witches' cats.
Cold dark nights
As autumn falls
Gives way to 'winter's cold'.

Sheila A Waterhouse

LOVERS IN AUTUMN

Leaves display their autumn gold,
  Wisps of smoke adorn the air,
My love, when spring returns
  Will you be there . . .
        Will you be there?

Misty mornings,
  Sunlight on a tranquil sea,
Summer ends its halcyon days,
  And so perchance must we.

The gradual hush of twilight
  Reflects the peace we share,
My love, when spring returns
  Shall we be there . . .
        Shall we be there?

J M Armstead

DAHLIAS

In the garden
The disordered dahlias
Droop like fading lamps,
Lighting the gloom of October,
Petals curled back,
Torn satin soaked by the rain,
Exposing the nipple,
The cold green breast
Of the flower.

Phantom faces in the dusk,
On the brink of November,
Month of withered flowers -
Rotted the crimson velvet,
Shredded the yellow silk,
Like curtains from a bedroom
Where one never slept,
Chamber of fantasy
Vacated long ago.

In depths of sleep
In the December night
The velvet glows again,
A finger touches
Unfading silk -
A known, loved face -
And all that is longed for is found,
In a late dream,
Before dawn.

But in the garden,
The tall brown ghosts of the dahlias,
Facing winter.

Dorothy Buyers

SEPTEMBER

September brings the changes
That is how it seems.
For in my life -
In this month -
So much has happened
In the passing years!
Changing scenes and occupations
Changing thoughts and attitudes.
All seem to come -
In September!
But September is the month of
                              newness -
New terms in schools and colleges
                          and universities!
So maybe this is why
September should be -
The start of a new year -
As in the Jewish calendar
When near this time a new year starts -
According to God's word!
So after rest and relaxation -
In the summer months -
We feel refreshed to start anew
When September comes!

Christina Miller

SEASON'S DELIGHT

Through misty haze the morning breaks
  And dew is left to linger
Upon those many coloured leaves that tremble and shimmer
  Gilded by the early frost they glint and shine
Ripened fruits ready for picking
  This the season of harvest time
This is the seasons with a flair no artist could ever compare
  Resplendent in this season filled with colour
Crowned by nature as your true beauty all discover

Walkways paved with carpets of leaves
  In their display of colours
Late blooming flowers add to this scene
  As the sun rays filter their bowers
Trees look gaunt as their leaves are shed
  Many stand out menacingly as we fear and dread
Brandishing their branches like spikes reaching out to cling
  As if to delay autumn's offering

Wood smoke essence twirls and combines as it pervades
  Decayed leaves are cremated
Into heaps their ashes are displayed
  For nutritional scattering the earth will be inundated
Oh autumn of delight and splendour
  This season of renown
Resplendent in nature's apparel
  To me every time you win your crown

R D Hiscoke

AUTUMN DREAMS

Beautiful bountiful autumn - season of sensual fulfilment -
Trapped 'twixt summer and winter -
Displaying a panoply of golden wonderment!
Palms out-stretched each single leaf lingering longingly
Wanting to stay bright green but knowing each tendril
Must be stripped to the bone -
Changing the face of Mother Earth
The first to fall displaying an artist's pallet
Of different shades and hues through from pale green to yellow
To brown to red - to be finally tossed in an ever-increasing
                                              turbulent wind -
Onto the ground to be carelessly breathlessly crunched underfoot
Cremated in gutters by hoards of children's green wellies!

Telegraph wires are a-buzzing weighed down by swarms of swifts
Swallows, starling chitter-chattering away
Conveying a communal spirit of caring togetherness
Consistently throughout deserts of despair
And troughs of despond!
As I wish them God speed a safe journey there and back
I think what an example they set for humankind
And trust my sand martins will return to honour us
With their personal visit next year
Where the nest will remain undisturbed . . .

Paula Fox

EVERY LEAF A SOUL

I watch the leaves fall
Every leaf a soul.

A pattern on the pavement
Only to be tramped away.

Each leaf a colour of hope
Worth more than all the gold.

Each leaf born to die -
As my auntie too -
Who cannot see this ever again.

I will remember with sadness
Each fall.

Terry Lane

The Glade

He lay there in anticipation
bare like the autumn trees around him.
The crinkly leaves formed a greeny
russet blanket to caress his body.
There was an autumn nip in the air
which kept his ardour in check.
All was quiet and peaceful in the glade until
a rustle and a crunch.
Then she came -
as naked as the tree bark.
She joined him on the leaf carpet
and as their love mingled
the blackbird sang to his mate
and the autumn leaves continued to fall.

Sarah Diskin

A WINDOW WITH A VIEW

A few socks, a lone, dark, heavy shirt blows in the wind
Dancing on the clothes pegs, struggling to be free.
A cold sun shines for a few minutes, then is hidden.
The pale, amber tipped clouds are floating high in the sky,

Shrubs are swaying to and fro, round and round they go,
The day is fierce, a few leaves have fallen, nature is dying.
No not dying, resting, dozing before the sleep of winter.
Skeleton-like plants holding on yet time for them to rest.

Some torn from their roots, rolling, jumping, tossed this way and that
Bouncing against strong statue-like shrubs, defiantly holding on.
This is shrub time, they are hardy and enjoy their role
Sporting berries and flowers, keeping strong roots in the soil.

Blow, blow wind, shake the dust off the old year's growth,
Reveal the buds to come when this bleak season is over.
Life will start again, now resting time is here, tidy, clear away.
Dear summer is gone, the earth is now preparing to sleep.

Betty Broom

THE QUALITY OF TREES

A sudden gust of wind has shaken free
The gold and auburn leaves from nearby trees;
With feather lightness floating to the ground
Like showers of confetti for a bride
They settle in bright patterns on the lawn.
New conkers burst with life each prickled case
And cast their treasures down upon the path
Adorning it in clusters plump and sleek
As children come to gather them with glee.
Although there is a freshness in the breeze
The sun still radiates caressing warmth
And bathes the scene in autumn's radiance.
It lights the poplars with a burnished bronze,
Instils a richness in the silver birch
That shimmers in the brilliance of its rays,
But soon the time will come when days are grey,
When trees, though lovely still, stark-naked stand
So some will feel a sadness in the air
That fleeting summer is no longer here.
When one has reached the autumn of one's life
There may be sorrow and a sense of loss
Unless one has the quality of trees,
No longer looking back with deep regret
Nor dreading winter days that lie ahead
But letting go and moving with the flow
By being present, knowing how to be.

Anne Greenhow

AUTUMN

His materials spread before Him,
The supreme Artist is at work -
Manipulating,
Moulding
Necklaces of gold,
Bracelets of copper,
Rings of fire,
Around every hill and knoll.

Until, at length, furnace-fading,
The flakes fall free,
Blowing and swirling in autumn's winds -
A memory of ephemeral radiance.

Joy Morton

PAST PRIME OF LIFE

Wrinkly leaves blush as if they were young lovers
But, the penultimate season has a dying fall.

From equinox to solstice
Time makes its unstoppable orbit
To draw me to life's phase,
Before eternal winter,
Where I mentally weigh which fruit I leave in store
And from that fruit which seeds be strewn with faith
To yield full-ripened crops,
For by our fruit we shall all be known.

Unlike the dogged farmer,
I will never reap my own harvest
Yet, through the autumn of my being,
Hope can daily thrive.

David Sewell Hawkins

AUTUMN MORNING

Gold, the soft gold of morning,
Warm on plough and stubble,
Pours down on moistened fields.
Long are the morning shadows
Cast by trees and hedgerows.
Bright red are the hips and haws.
Gold on the backs of horses,
And on towers of churches,
Gold on girls' hair and faces,
Gold on barns and houses,
Of worth that is never debased,
Comes in uncounted profusion
From a vault that is never exhausted.

Angus Sinclair

LOVE AFFAIR

It's a love affair with the lands of history and legend
Mountains rise forever bathed in coloured shadows of the hours
As gossamer mist lifts mountains surrender their charms
Golden gorse mingle with heather clad moors
Amongst rustic bracken sheep wander through fields to tarns
Landscapes changing to their autumnal gowns
Rich in colours of earth and fire
Pine forests steeped in a world of enchantment
Where once lived maidens, knights, pages and sires
Trickling streams meander into raging falls
And time swims against the ever-changing tides
Words of love drift with haunting calls
Entwine yourself in the ribbons of history
With each hero and their dreams
Whispering love's sigh for lands of legends and mystery

Susan E Roffey

SUBMISSIONS INVITED
SOMETHING FOR EVERYONE

POETRY NOW 2003 - Any subject,
any style, any time.

WOMENSWORDS 2003 - Strictly women,
have your say the female way!

STRONGWORDS 2003 - Warning!
Opinionated and have strong views.
(Not for the faint-hearted)

All poems no longer than 30 lines.
Always welcome! No fee!
Cash Prizes to be won!

Mark your envelope (eg *Poetry Now*) **2003**
Send to:
Forward Press Ltd
Remus House, Coltsfoot Drive,
Peterborough, PE2 9JX

**OVER £10,000 POETRY PRIZES
TO BE WON!**

Judging will take place in October 2003